My Favorite Relaxing Coloring Book
- Dinosaurs 1 -

This book is a wonderful addition to your coloring library. A perfect gift for school children, college students, or adults who enjoy coloring.

It is much easier way to reduce stress then going to a gym.

NOTE: While these pages are good quality, sometimes pens/gels/markers can bleed. I recommend using a Bleed Protector (a piece of cardstock for example) under the coloring page to protect your book.

The drawings are copyright protected. The drawings are intended for your personal use only. You are not permitted to sell any of these images in any way. You may post the final coloring via social media, but you must acknowledge the artist in your posting. Thank you..

All Rights reserved Mike Peterson © 2015

Cover Page Colored by Maria S Garza

Printed by FCB Books

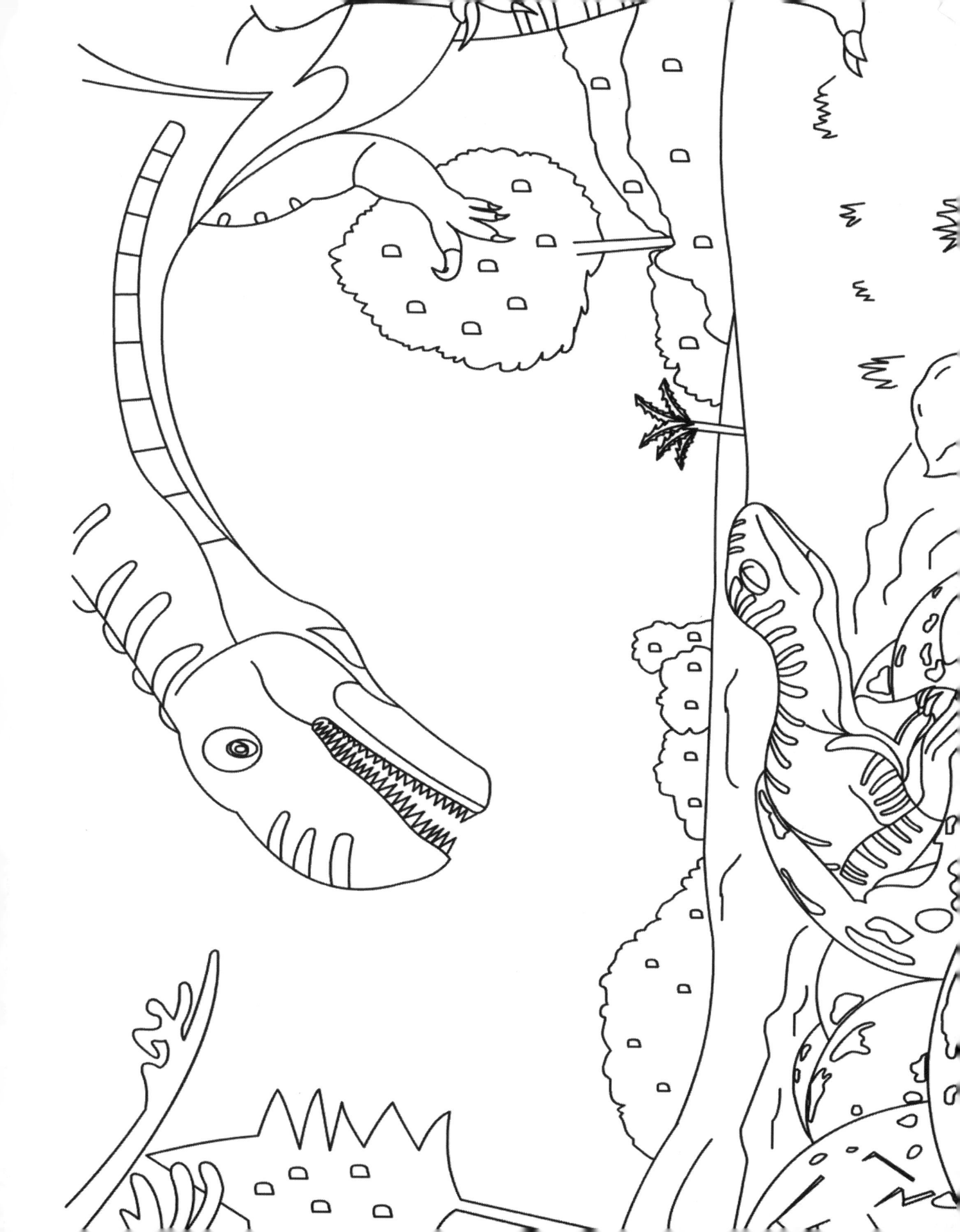

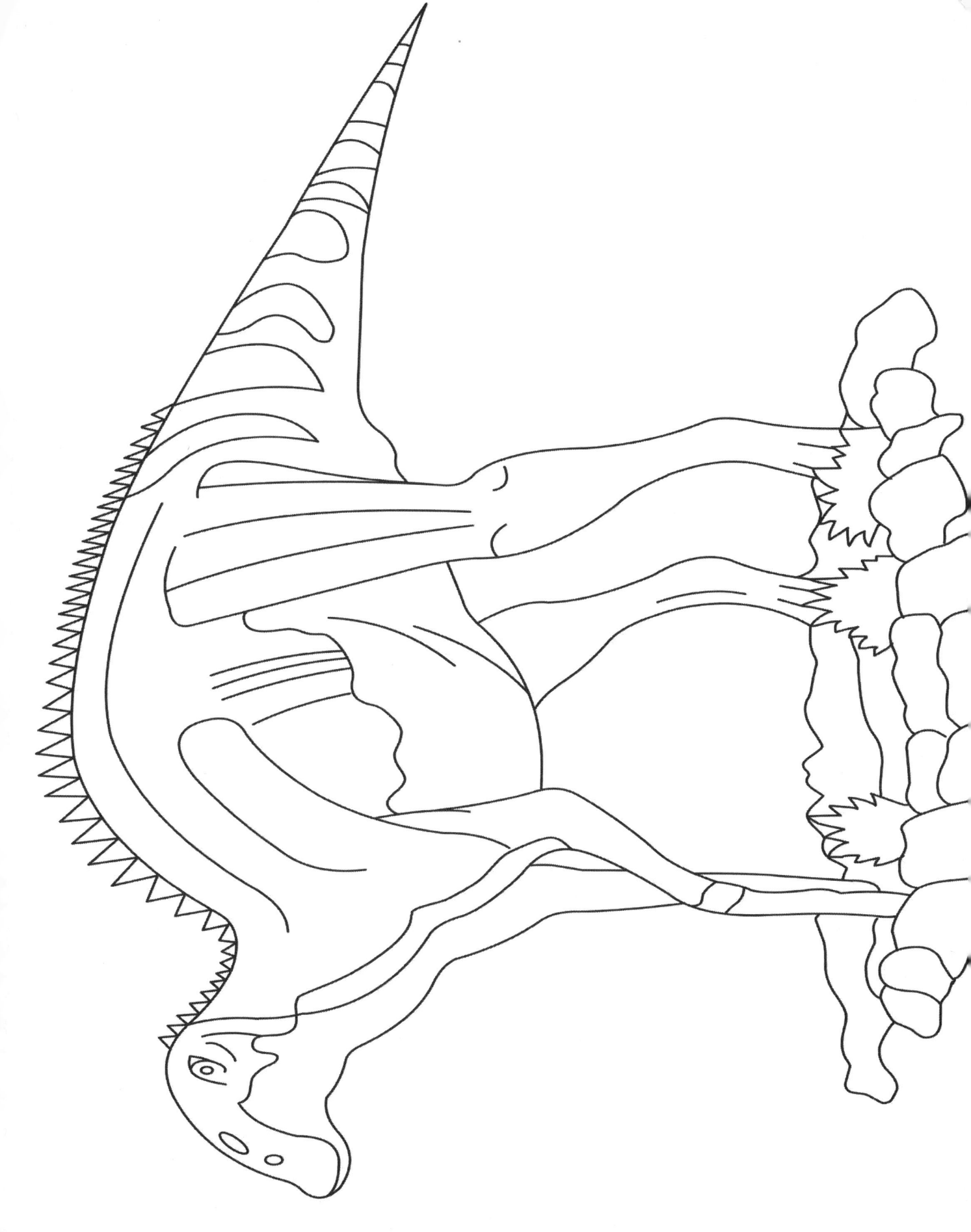

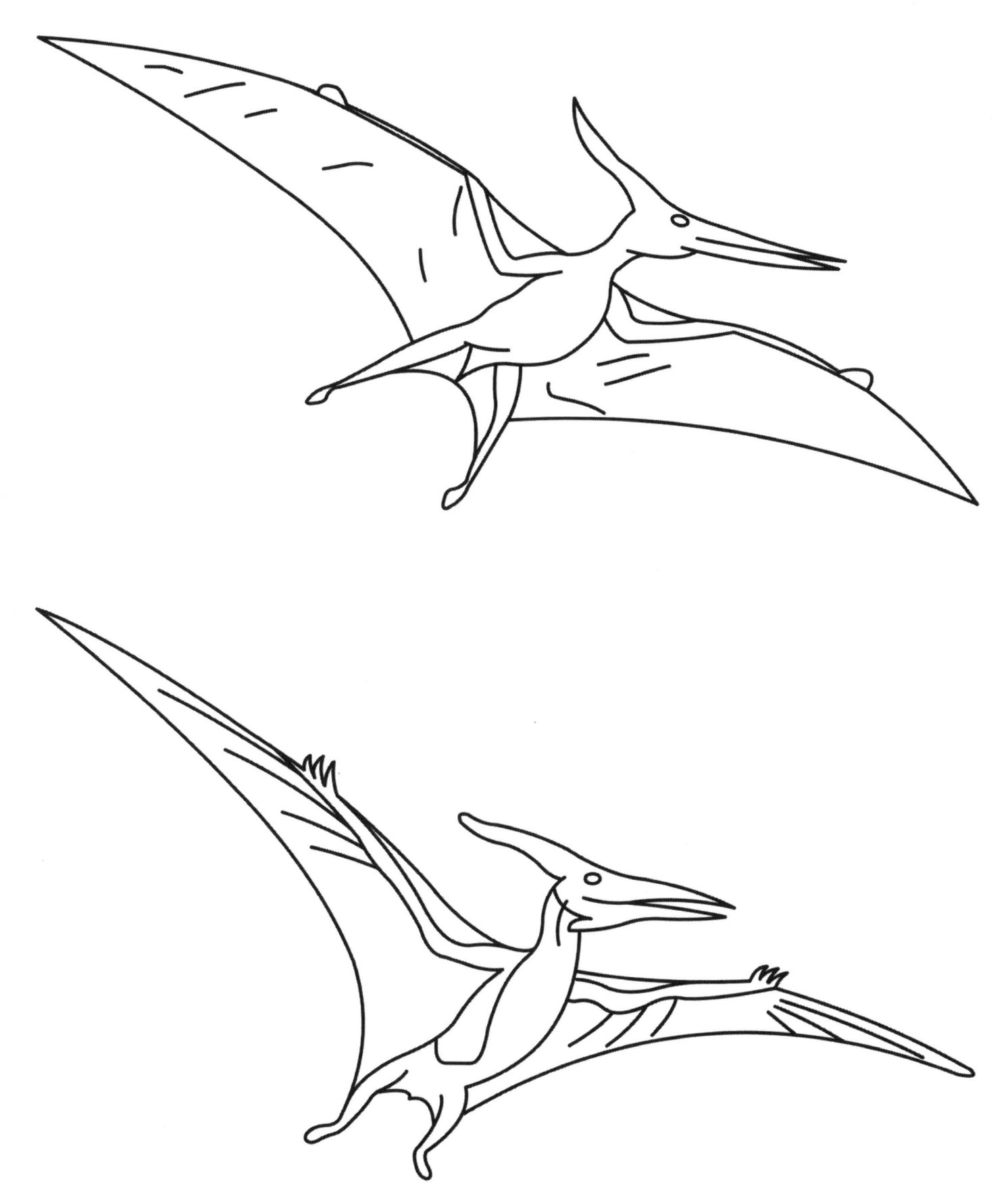

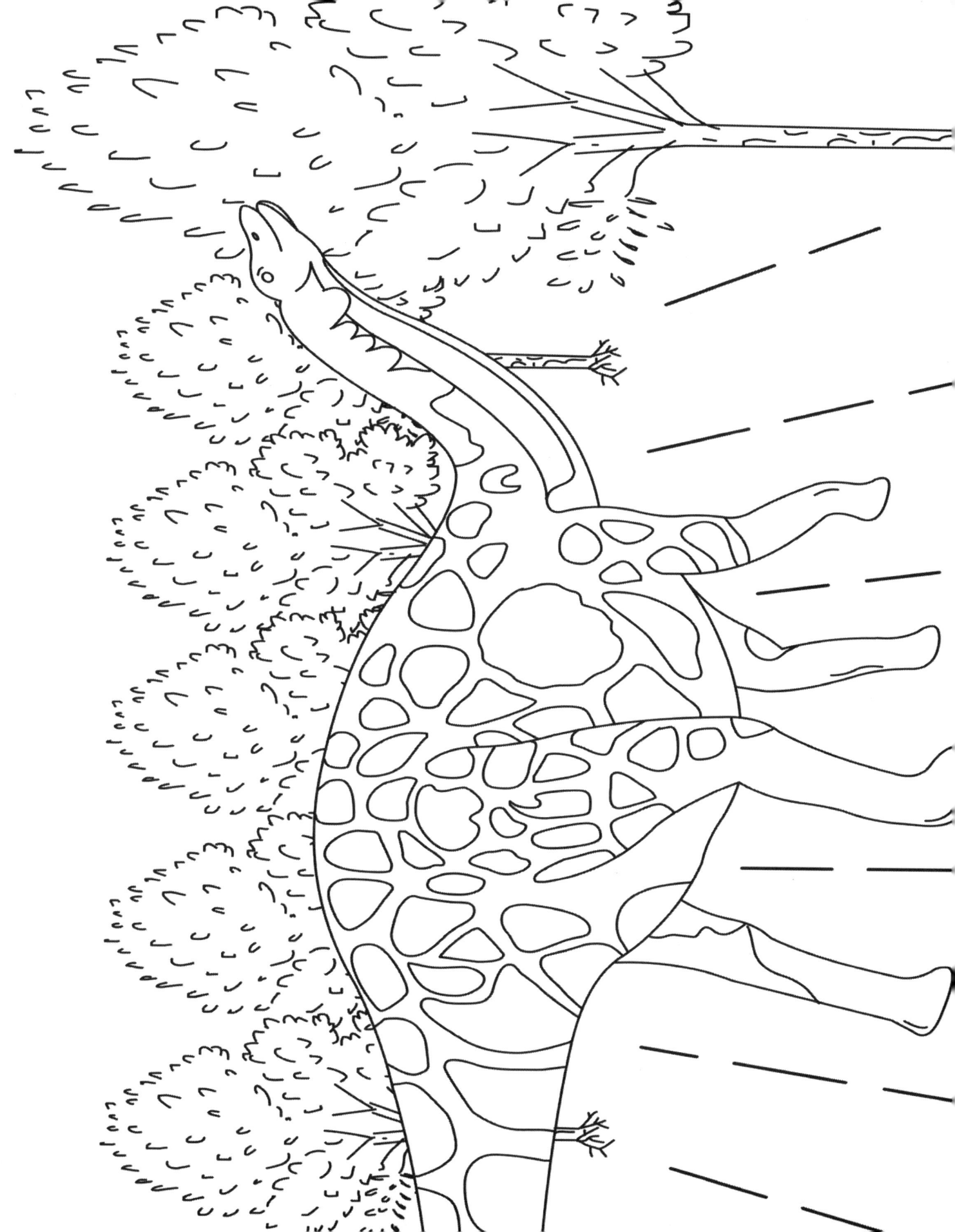

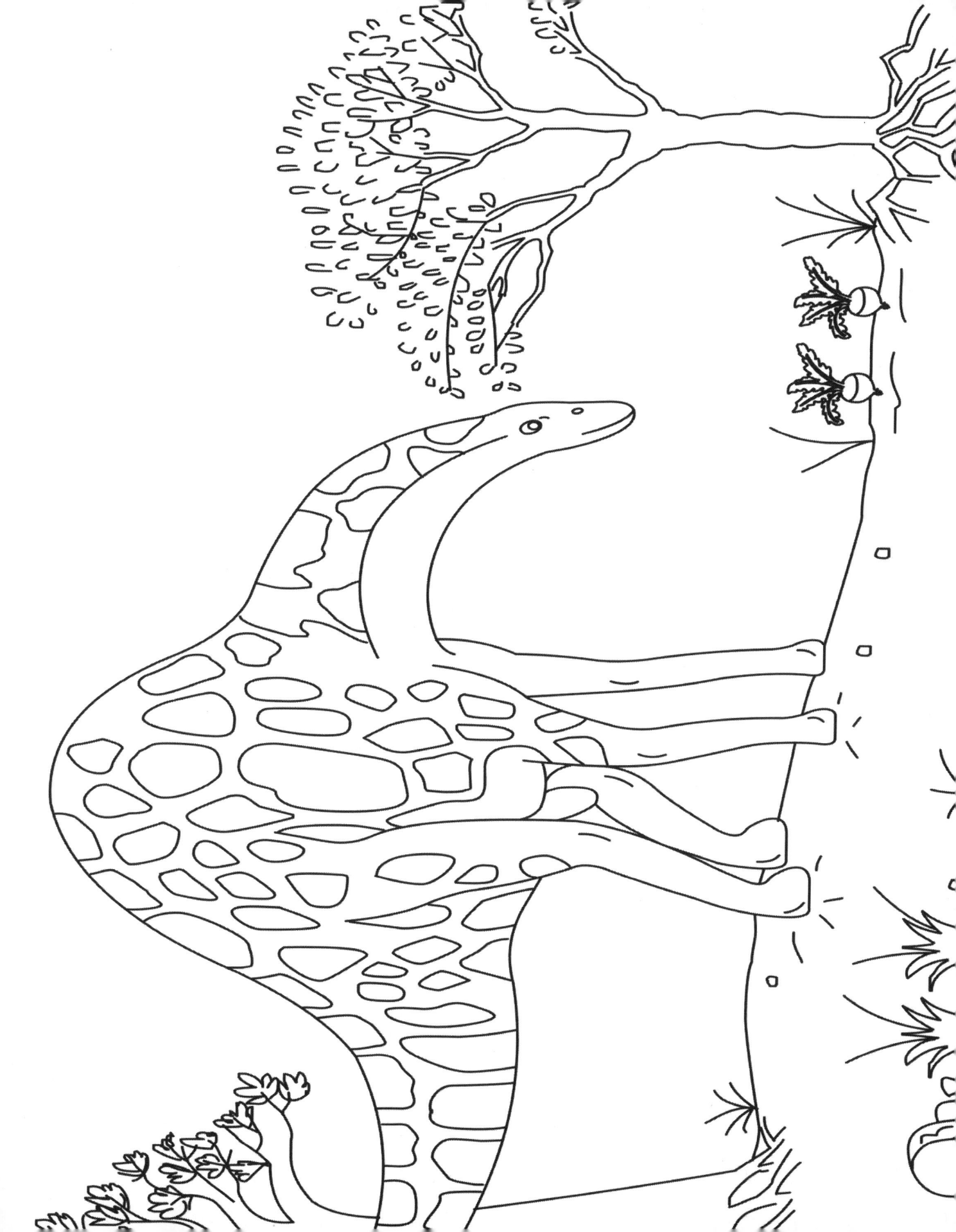

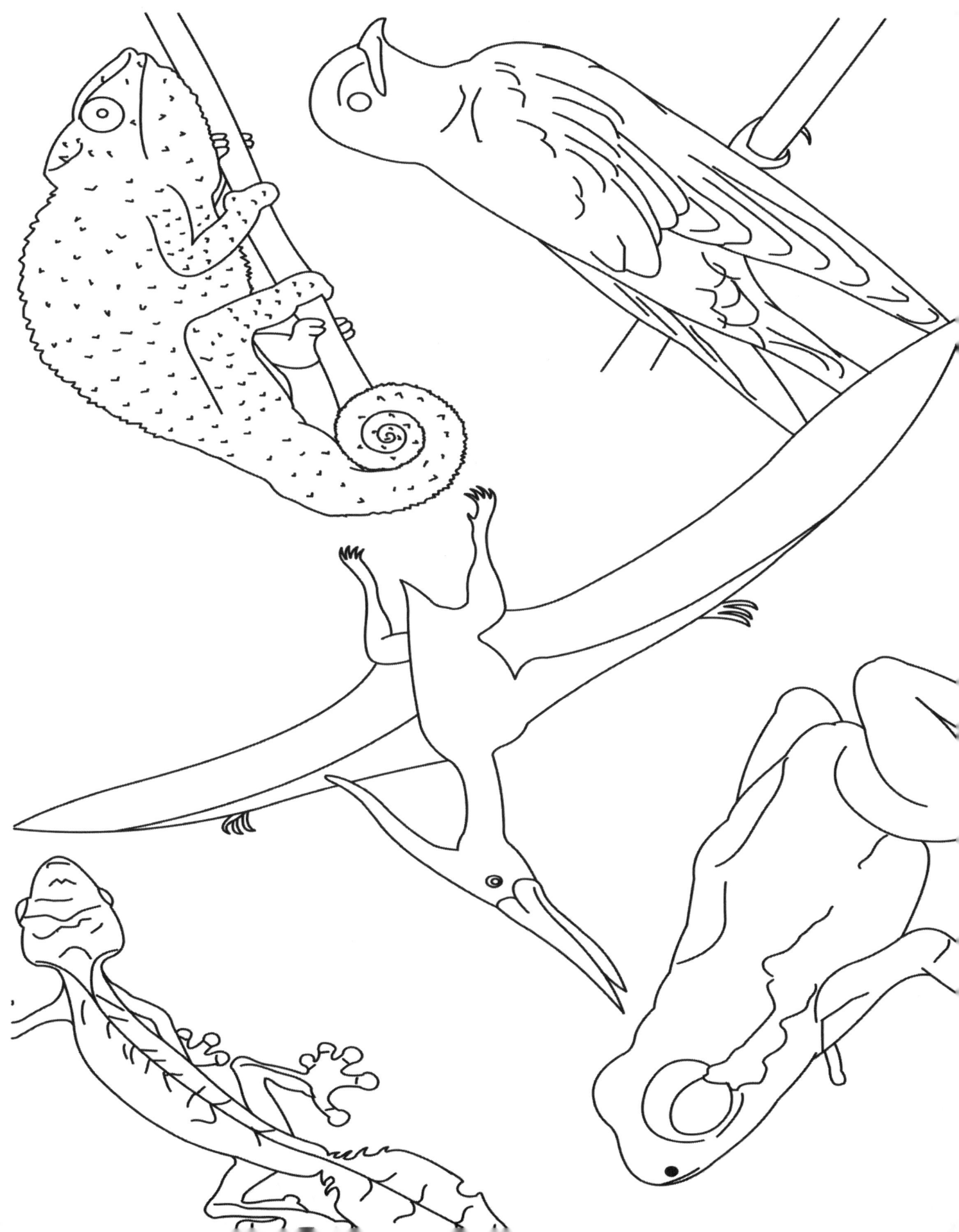

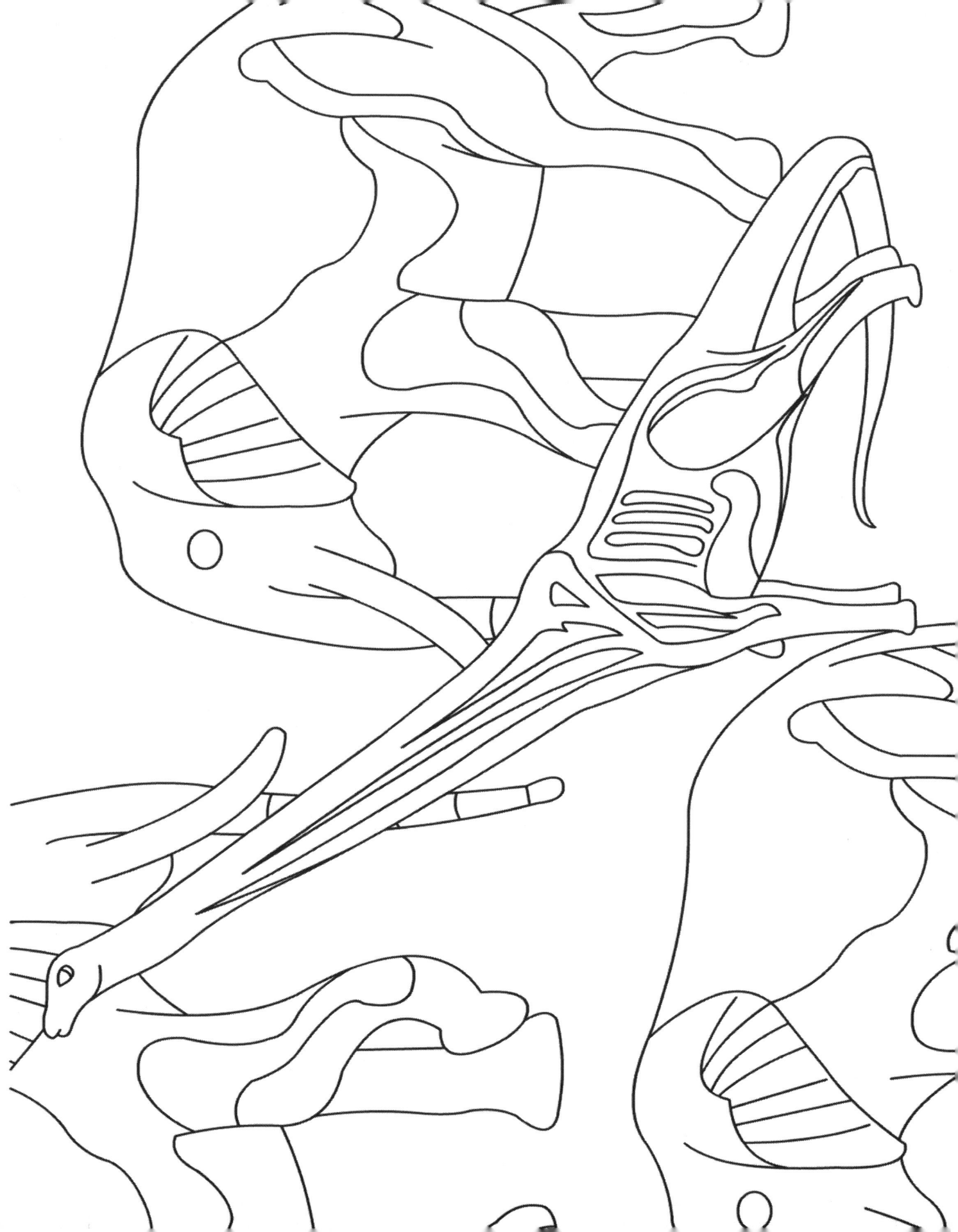

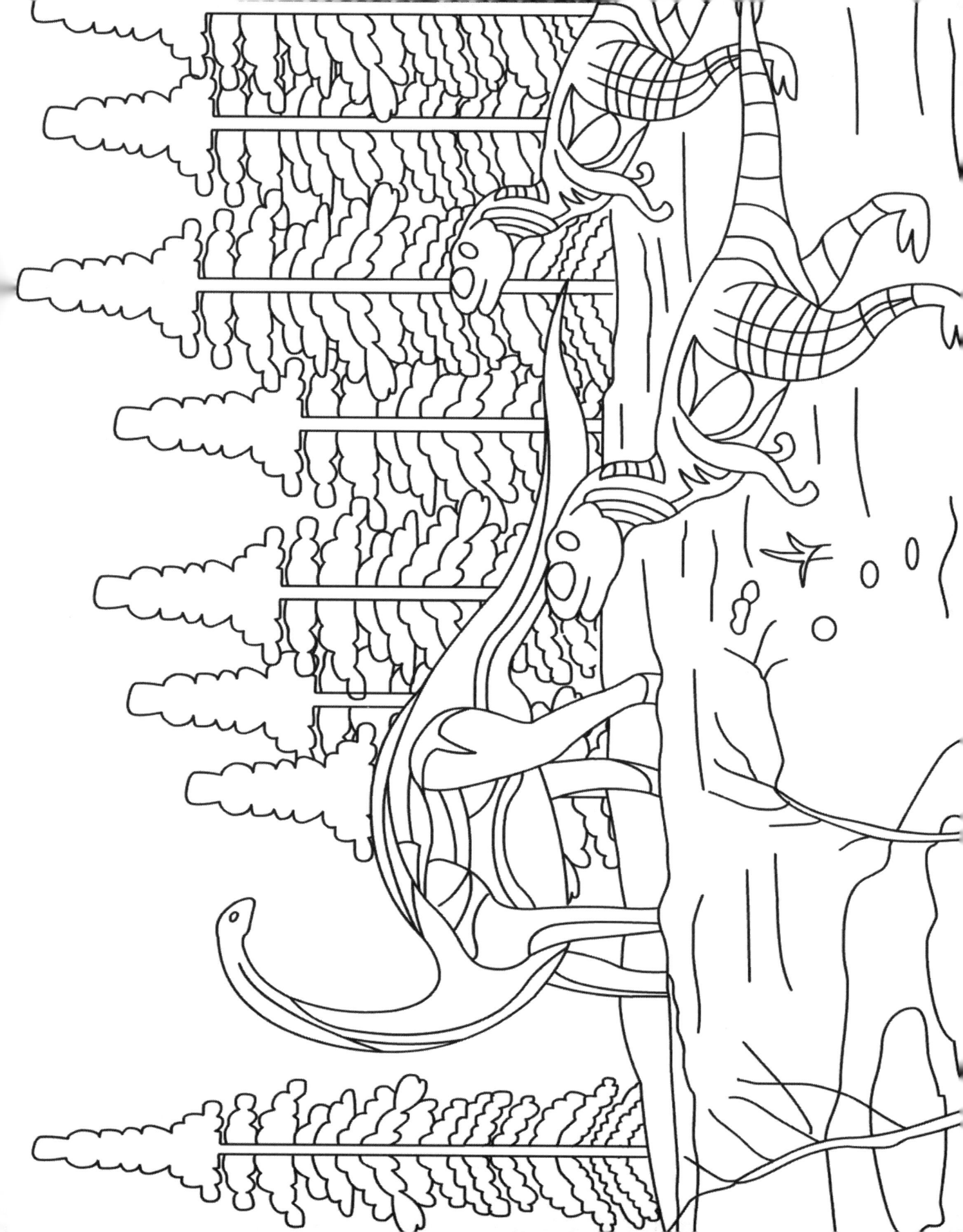

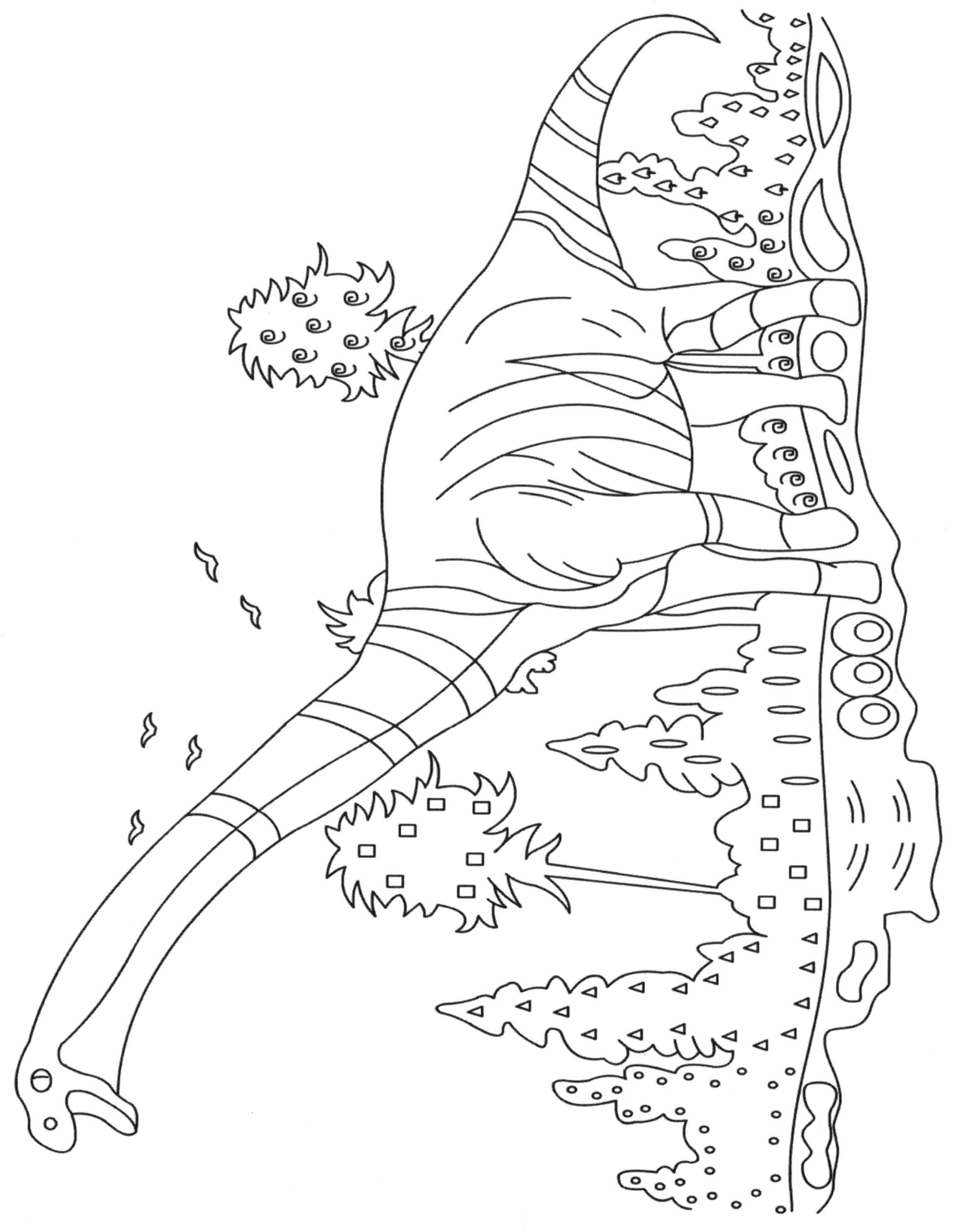

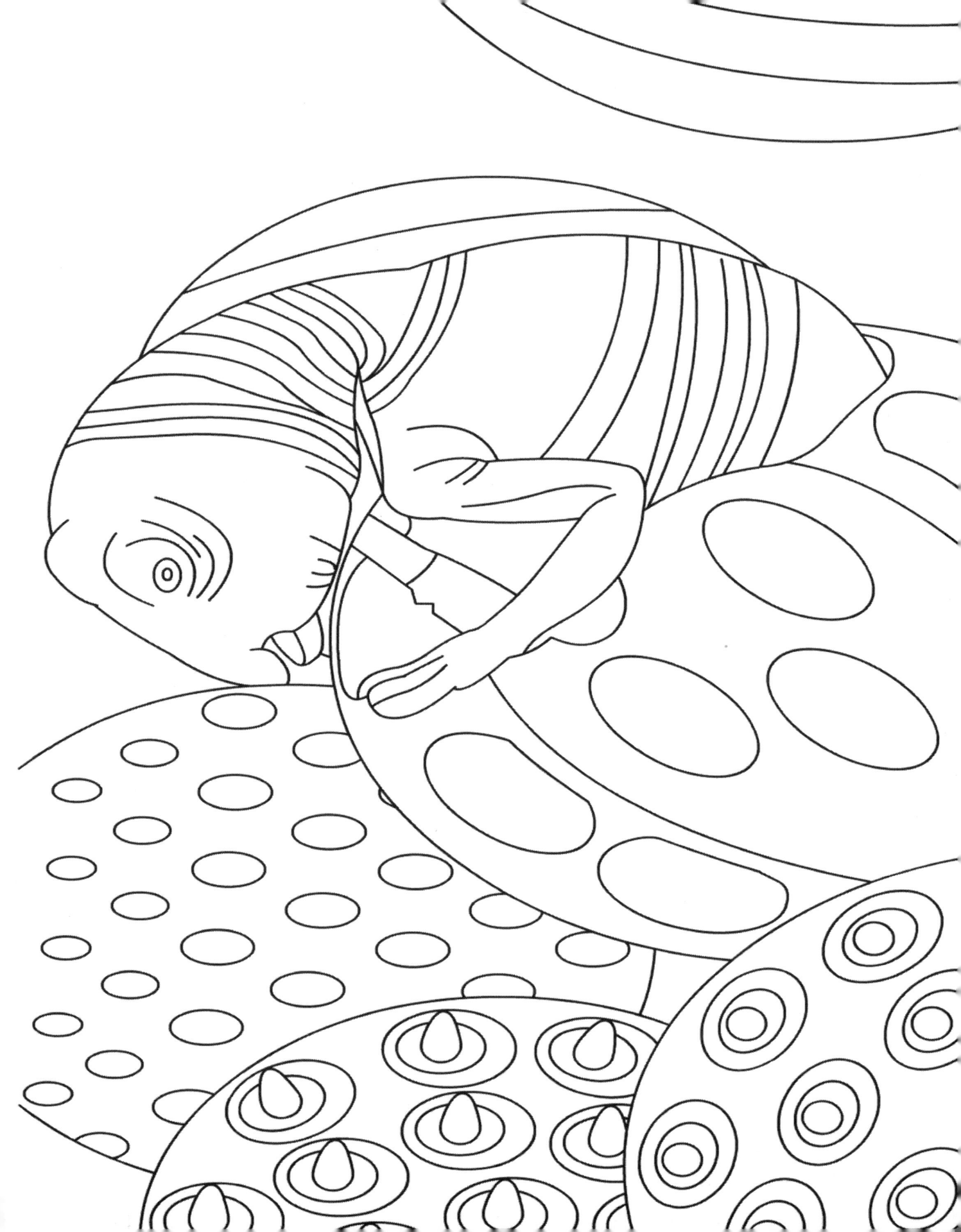

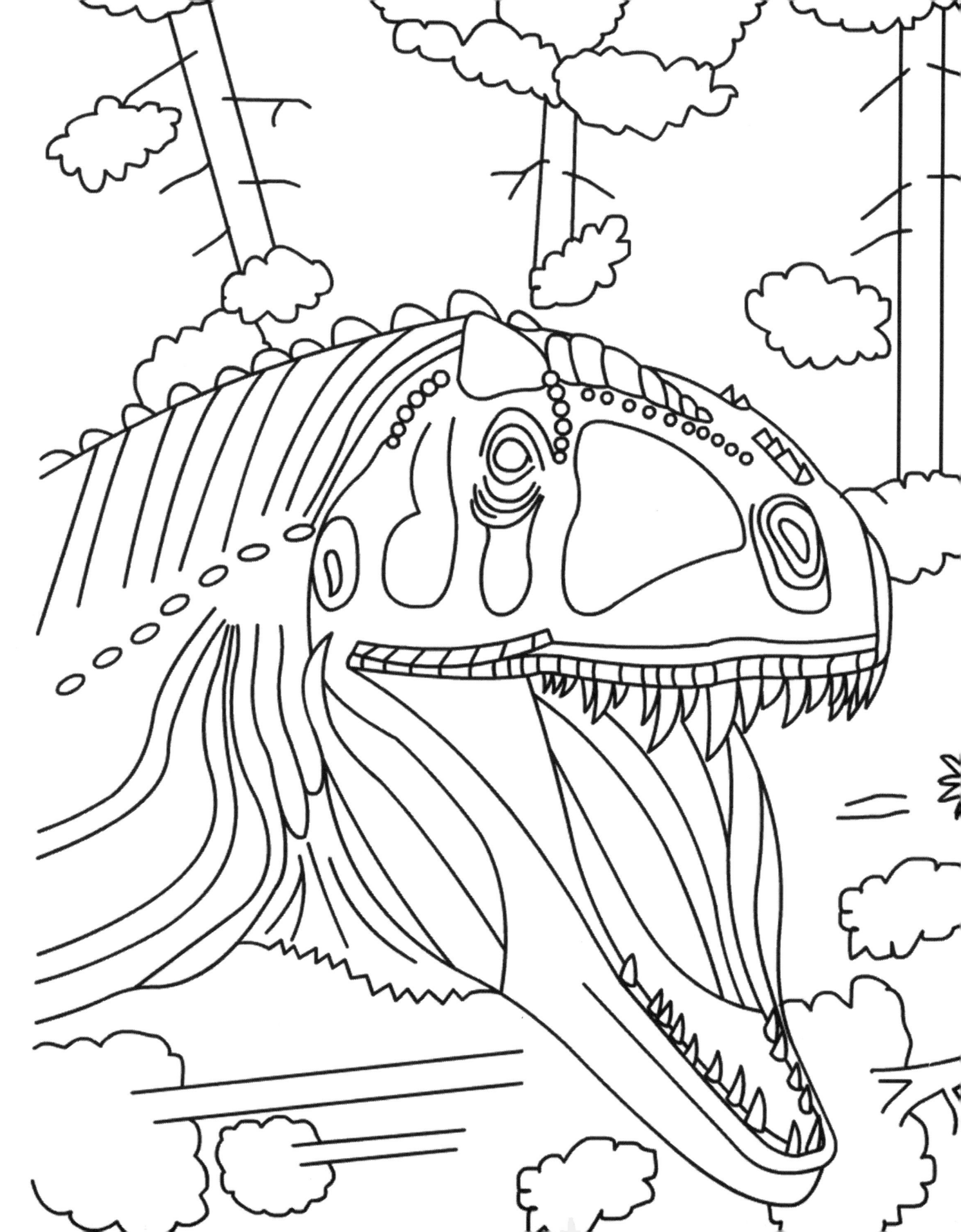

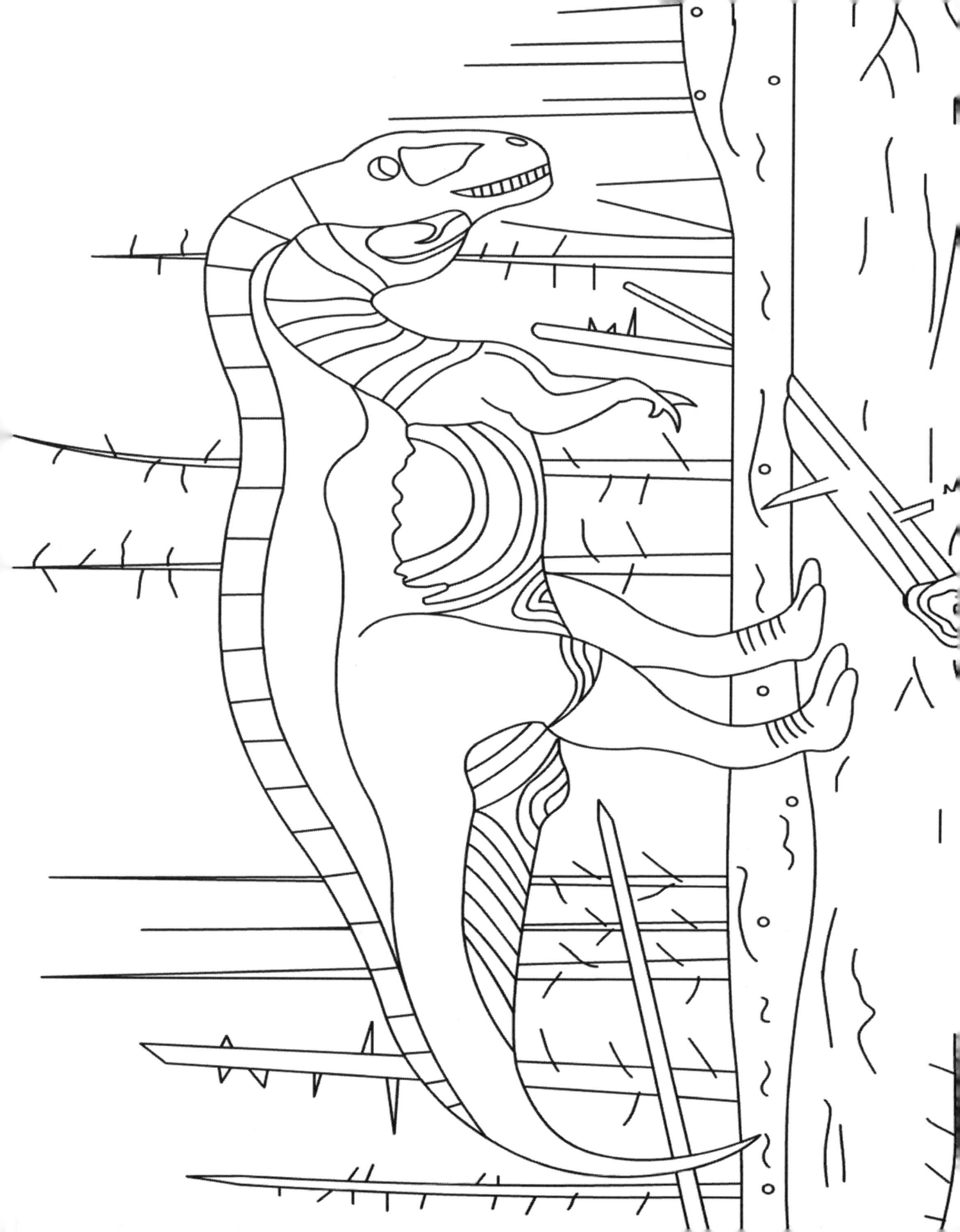

Made in the USA
Middletown, DE
12 December 2015